— AUTHOR'S NOTE —

It is my deep belief that if you have picked up this book, it is because this is your story.

If you are standing at a crossroads, struggling to understand the meaning behind a life event that has brought you to your knees

— let this story be your own —

Allow your mind to be drawn to the moments where you have been called to your greatest darkness and your greatest light.

Truth speaks only one language and always leads us home to ourselves, so walk boldly into the story of your own becoming.

— Some will call this fiction —

— others will simply answer the call —

Will You Dance?

Will You Dance?

Annette
Childs-Oroz, Ph.D.

Afterword by
Raymond A. Moody, Jr., M.D., Ph.D.

THE
wandering
feather
PRESS

Will You Dance?
Annette Childs-Oroz, Ph.D.

ISBN 0-9718902-0-X

Library of Congress Control Number: 2002092479

10 9 8 7 6 5 4 3 2

THE
wandering
feather
PRESS

774 Mays Blvd. #10-488
Incline Village, NV 89451

www.willyoudance.com

ORIGINAL ARTWORK by Karen A. Kreyeski

ACKNOWLEDGMENTS
Cover Concept by AnnieMation.com
Cover Collage from original paintings for this book by Karen A. Kreyeski

Additional backgrounds by Paul Cirac
WHITE SAGE STUDIOS

Design and prepress by Paul Cirac at WHITE SAGE STUDIOS
Published in association with Greg Nielsen, CONSCIOUS BOOKS 1-800-322-9943

Printed and Bound in Singapore by TIEN WAH PRESS

To
my little ones
Sutter and Delaney
whose blue eyes were there to greet me
when life had dropped me to my knees.

– and –

to
Felix and Andy and Sara
who walked so very softly
into our world
and
into our hearts.

Destiny sat quietly fingering his long gray beard,
having just convened a meeting with six hooded figures.
He, of course, had a legion of followers,
but it was these six who were very often
the messengers that he sent out for the journey.

He glanced out the Windows of Time
and watched three
of the hooded figures veer off to the left.
He smiled to himself, knowing that for the souls ready
to receive these three visitors,
the Dance
would soon begin

He lifted himself from a chair that rocked gently to the
rhythms of fate. As he draped his hood over thick sterling
hair that fell soft like starlight against his neck,
he tilted his head a bit to the side, trying to capture
the distant strains of an ancient melody
that played softly in the back of his mind . . .
Once again, it was time for him to open the gate,
and let
the Dance
begin.

Destiny walks beside us
like a silent companion . . .
Neither stepping ahead or falling behind,
but instead meeting us stride for stride
as we meander
the landscapes of our lives.

Silently standing by with the patience of
our own shadow on a bright summer's day . . .
quietly **Destiny** waits . . .

He often remains elusive
only to step boldly
from the shadows one day,
calmly announcing his presence
with quiet conviction.

It is then
that we make the choice
of who we will be in this lifetime—
. . . Will we cower and shrink
from what beckons us forward
. . . or will we step boldly forward
to answer
the
call?

And what now follows
is a story.
This may be your story,
it may be the story of a stranger.
It may be the story of your future
or
the story of your past . . .

At some point this has been
or will be your story,
for it is a universal tale.
It began long, long ago
and when your heart
hears this tale,
you too
will remember that you
came here
to dance . . .

... It seemed like an ordinary day,
but years later
when we looked back upon it,
our memories insist that it was unusually
still in the world that late summer morning.
Whether time has created our notions,
or our notions
have created time,
we each seem to remember
a slow motion quality to that day ...
like the clock was dragging its hands a bit,
wishing to let us
savor every last moment of our lives
before that knock on the door came,
and our journey began ...

Tap . . . tap . . . tap . . .

like the lazy thump
that comes from the
tail of a half sleeping dog
who long ago
gave up notions
of chasing anything
other than its own
black and white dreams . . .

Harder now,

tap . . .

tap . . .

tap . . .

The knock on the door,
was
Destiny.
We had no choice but to answer.
Before us,
stood three hooded figures,
their faces we could not see.
It took only moments for us to realize
who it was that stood before us . . .

On our doorstep
stood
Change,
and behind
Change
stood
Fear,
and next to
Fear
was
Loss.

We
tried
to
explain
that surely they

must

be

mistaken . . .

but they stood firm,
until
there was nothing left to do
but invite
them
in . . .

The first to enter was
Change.
With her she brought a gust of wind
that swept away
all of the familiar things
we had known in our world. . .
We watched helplessly
as the life we had known
dissipated
like a tiny stream of smoke
which rises from a candle,
whose flame has just been extinguished . . .

We stood in quiet consternation,
watching life as we had known it
rise in that smoke,
growing more and more diffuse,
until it finally
disappeared
altogether.

Next to enter were
Fear
and
Loss.
They moved as one,
and entered
arm in arm.
And with them came a strange silence . . .
a silence that was born
out of the inability to hear
anything but the truth . . .

The truth moved through us
like a ripple moving through a placid lake . . .
concentric rings pushing out from the center
expanding until finally merging back
into the vastness from which they came . . .

We felt our knees buckle a bit,
as the waves of truth rocked us
gently from side to side . . .

It was
very, very quiet
for a long while.
We were
held in rapt attention
of all that was unfolding around us.
We watched,
with wide eyed wonder,
as truth rushed in like a wave,
filling up
all of the fractures
that the winds of
Change
had laid bare.

If time moved at all,
it could have been
minutes
or
years

as we were tossed on the

stormy seas

of
Change,
Fear,
and
Loss.

The currents of surrender washed over us,
time and time again . . .
until at last we were delivered
into the mercy
of our unbidden guests . . .

And then like a great howling wind
who has spent its fury,
the tempest stopped
and before us,
becalmed
once again,
stood this trio,
of
Change,
Fear,
and
Loss.

Having been
granted safe passage,
there we stood
in the quiet that follows the storm.

It took quite a long while
for us to raise our eyes up,
to dare and take the chance
of peering into the eyes
of these dark hooded figures
who had entered our lives uninvited.

Yet, once we became willing to
look upon their cloaked faces,
we found a curious mixture of things
that caused us to visually grasp at them,
the way a child grasps at the string of a balloon
as it slips quickly from the hand . . .
Their features were indistinct,
like a vapor . . .
swirling and mesmerizing,
falling into themselves and spilling outward
all at the same time.
They were hypnotic in their presence,
and we were compelled to return their gaze
for many long moments.

An odd comfort fell around us
like a heavy wool blanket . . .
offering both burden and warmth.
Contained neatly
within this odd comfort
was a dull ache
as we remembered how life had been
before
Change's
winds had blown through
our lives
and taken
all that was familiar away . . .

There was a catch in our throats,
as if we had just inhaled the hot dusty air
that hangs in an attic
that has been too long closed,
as we remembered
the happy laughter
that had gone away
like

a

raindrop
hitting
a hot summer sidewalk,
when
Fear
and
Loss
had surrounded us
with the silence of truth . . .

As we became accustomed to the presence
of these three,
we slowly resumed a shadow
of what many would call living . . .
We sat together at dinner each night,
aware that although
we had not set out any extra dinner plates,
there were three beings
who sat at the table alongside of us.
Silently they sat,
. . . waiting . . .
for what we did not know.
And then one day
without a word to one another,
we simply took their hands . . .
for it seemed
at the time,
there was nothing else to do . . .

To our surprise
there was a strange comfort
in embracing them,
and as we held fast to their hands
they began to gently tug at us . . .
tugging at our borders,
and making us

s t r e t c h

The three of them
were not always gentle,
but
mercy was their close companion.
Like the potter mixing clay,
using the dust of our old withered dreams,
and
the water born of our tears,
they kneaded,
and worked,
blended and twisted,
pressed and shaped
each of us,
until we were
no longer
that
which we used to be . . .

Like water that is unleashed
into the intricate mosaic
of a long dry creek bed,
we released ourselves,
spilling
into all that was calling us forward . . .
expanding into places
we dared go
only because
we held the hands
of these mysterious strangers.

Soon
we were like cats
sprawling in the summer sun,
stretching ourselves
lazily and without resistance.

Gone was the container
of our old world.
Gone were the borders of a
neatly
ordered life . . .

And carried on the wind were
quiet accolades from the Universe,
gently nudging us forward . . .
reassuring us
that to
sift through the rubble of a broken life,
builds a soul strong . . .
strong
like the mighty and towering oak.

All the while,
we lived
in a world that
had grown
empty
and
silent . . .

Empty
because the winds that
Change
brought with her
had cleared out
all that was familiar,
and
silent
because
Fear
and
Loss
had brought with them
the hushed silence of truth . . .
And truth it seems is
oh
so
quiet . . .
usually only making a whisper,
if making
any sound
at
all . . .

Oddly enough,
the emptiness
was somehow vibrant,
and this void,
it was buzzing with the hum of possibility . . .
the possibility
of all
that wanted to become
in our world.

And the silence,

the silence
held within it
the sound
of a still
small
voice . . .
a voice
called to life
by these strangers
whose names were
Change
Fear
and **Loss** . . .

Emptiness and silence
enveloped us
warm and dark like a womb.

It was there
in the soft dark belly of truth
that we took shelter,
while we let ourselves and
a life we had cherished die
and learned to live again.

. . . And then once again,
Destiny
called
and
there was
a
knock on the door.

Change,
Fear,
and
Loss
exchanged sly smiles
as we rose
to
answer
the
call.

Standing before us were
Hope
Faith
and
Joy.

Change,
Fear,
and
Loss,
gently greeted these three.
It was apparent
they were old friends . . .
the kind of friends that went way back,
comrades who
needed no fancy greetings
or well-oiled words.

They were
the kind of friends
that came together like watercolors,
running into each other and
birthing a whole new color,
just from letting
their edges merge.

With hushed words they spoke,
glancing at us every so often.
Their conversation was brief,
yet their words were heavy,
heavy like the fog
which lies on top of valleys
in early autumn.

Of the three new guests,
Joy
seemed to be the most conversant.
Stepping forward
with the authority of an orator,
Joy
thanked us
for having prepared a space for them,
and for offering shelter
to their traveling companions.
We
looked upon
Joy
quizzically ,
unsure of what she spoke.

Seeing our uncertainty
Joy
quickly explained
that in the ways of the Universe
Change
Fear
and
Loss
always
travel
ahead
to carefully prepare a place for
Hope
Faith
and
Joy.

We invited them in,
and watched with wonder
as these six cloaked figures
joined hands
and
began to move
in a deliberate
and
intricate way.

A strange quiet came upon us,
as our minds were
drawn to a
place
between worlds.
The veil of
things earthly fell away,
and a gossamer vision
spread before us
the way moonlight
spreads soft
across water.

Within each of the six beings
lay a treasure.
Gifts offered only to those who
make the hard journey
to wisdom's door.

With childlike eyes
we watched
as
these gifts were
offered
before us.

The first
to be offered
was the gift of
weaving.

Before us appeared
the shadowy apparition
of a weaver at the loom.
And knelt at the feet of this weaver
was
one who very gently guided this sacred cloth
as it emerged in soft billowy folds.

Meticulously they worked,
taking great care to
unravel the tangled strands
of a life come undone.
Silently taking
individual threads,
threads of change and fear and loss,
threads of hope and faith and joy,
merging them all
into
a single sacred fabric . . .
a fabric worthy
to swaddle
a delicate
newborn life.

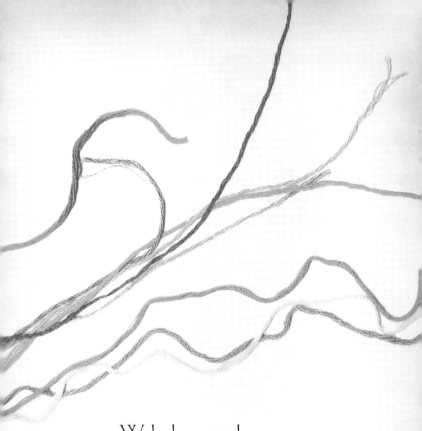

With the quiet eloquence
of a sunset,
we were shown how to weave
both the darkness
and the light
into the tapestry of our lives.

We soon
came to know
that the loom
upon which this fabric was woven,
was the loom of
silence,

and
as the fabric emerged
it was gathered gently
into a basket,
a basket made from
the willows of
truth.

And so . . . we came to know
that the weaving, yes
the weaving . . .

this was the gift
of **Fear**
and
Loss,
for
silence
and
truth
were the things that
trailed behind these two,
like streamers
waving in the wind . . .

The next gift
to be offered
was the gift of
breaking.
We watched
as a shudder
collectively moved through
the six of them.

They swayed in unison,
like a golden
field of wheat, caressed by
the invisible fingers
of the wind.

Gently
they each forgave
their own rigidity,
abandoning
the struggle to bend,
embracing
the strength to break
with grace.

We watched
as the six beings
silently
surrendered themselves
to the gift of
breaking.

We watched
as they each became softer,
as they each in some small way,
allowed the gift of breaking
to permeate them . . .

Fear
and
Loss
leaned heavily upon one another,
as the weight of breaking descended upon them.
Fear
gave a sigh with his out-breath,
while
Loss
took a sharp breath in,
as if
trying to capture
her companion's sigh
and hold it within her.

Breaking
came
from both
above and below
as
Faith
held her head up high
and stood
with a posture of majesty,
as she received
this difficult gift
with all of the dignity
she could muster.

Hope
simply
cradled the gift,
as if it were a child . . .
holding it gently
and rocking it back and forth.
There was
a gentle cadence to her rocking,
as if
she was panning for the gold
she knew
lay hidden
within the silt . . .

Joy
cast her gaze downward,
as breaking
burrowed deep within her.
We watched in silence
as a perfect teardrop . . .
slid quietly . . .
from beneath the hood of
Joy.

We watched
as that perfect crystalline teardrop fell,
falling with the quiet desperation
of a single drop of rain,
as it travels unceasingly
toward a parched and thirsty surface . . .

It tumbled
down
and down
and down,
gathering up years of dreams,
collecting them
as a child would collect seashells
while
walking along the beach . . .

Oh

so

slowly

that

teardrop

fell.

And at the moment
the teardrop
met its destination

we were
stunned and silent
as it shattered . . .

filling our ears
with the sound
of a thousand
broken dreams,
and filling our vision
with
a million points of
iridescent light
which rose up
from the fragments
like
the dust that dances
within a sunbeam . . .

We watched
as this
iridescent dust
swirled around
and through the six of them,

casting
an ethereal glow
as it
ebbed and flowed
with
their every movement.

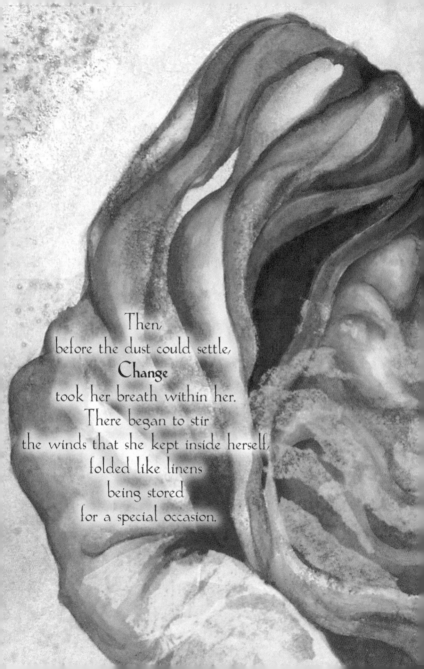

Then,
before the dust could settle,
Change
took her breath within her.
There began to stir
the winds that she kept inside herself,
folded like linens
being stored
for a special occasion.

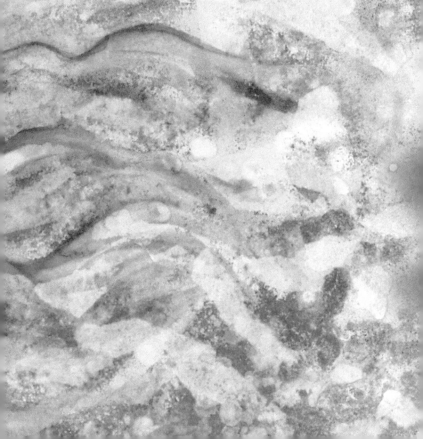

And
gently she blew . . .
blowing free the dust of broken dreams
releasing them
before they could settle
into any of the nooks and crannies
that life allows . . .

and so it was
that we
came to know that
breaking
was the gift of
Change . . .

For
to become whole,
we first must be broken
into pieces.
It is only
when we lay scattered in fragments,
that the light
can make
its way through us.

Just then,
from the corner of our vision
came the graceful arc
of a
beautiful creature in flight.

We were all transfixed
by this beautiful winged creature,
not quite an angel,
but being far from a bird.
It was a mixture of
clouds and feathers,
windows and mirrors . . .

Gracefully it danced
in the ether above us,
like a ribbon that trails
behind a kite,
darting playfully
in and out
the way a child plays at hide and seek . . .

Tucking
into a tight ball
only to unfurl with abandon,
like a flag
that is caught unaware
by a sudden gust of summer wind . . .

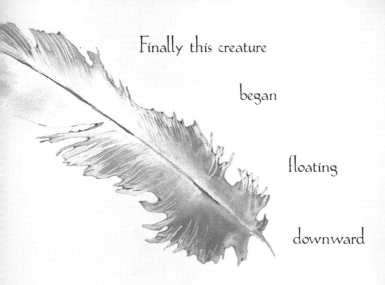

Finally this creature

began

floating

downward

with the grace that embodies
a fine white feather,
newly released from the
downy folds of a gosling.

Hope
stretched her hand outward,
and gently this beautiful
floating mixture
of light and air,
came to rest in her palm.

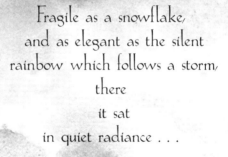

Fragile as a snowflake,
and as elegant as the silent
rainbow which follows a storm,
there
it sat
in quiet radiance . . .

There was a collective sigh,
as we
realized . . .

that this winged creature
perched before us,
was the exquisite
and delicate
gift
of
Hope.

For
Hope
from the moment
we first saw her,
contained a buoyancy that
allowed the hem of her garment
to float around her
the way mist hovers
above mountain lakes on cold
winter mornings.
For
it seemed to us,
that
Hope
never actually came into contact
with the ground
upon which she strode.

Then one of the six bent down,
and began to pull forward
an old and tarnished chest.
One could only vaguely
tell that it was a chest,
for its entire surface was encased
in a dense and dark matter
like the
uneven and harsh shell of an oyster.

With the deliberation of a sculptor
who can see a treasured carving
buried deep within
a block of stone,
this determined being
began to pick and work
at that
which entombed the chest.

The first piece
of this outer shell
to fall free
had edges so sharp that we stepped back
so as not to
risk cutting ourselves.
As we
peered down at the ragged edges
we could see the reflection
of our own misperceptions
staring back at us.

It was then
that we came to know
how it is
that our own illusions
cut us so deeply,
making bleed
that
which is home to both our
hearts
and our bones.

The next piece to fall
was heavy and dense.
It fell
with a thud,
it sat heavy
like a rock.
As we peered more intently
at the gnarled and twisted casing
that lay
on the ground before us,
we could clearly see
the fingerprints of bitterness
on the
craggy unforgiving surface.

Finally . . .
the rest of the shell fell
in various smaller pieces,
small bits
of cynicism,
flecks
of blame,
and
an occasional shard
of deceit.

As the chest
was released from the
dark embrace of this shell,
Faith
put her hands to her face.

. . . Like a mother
peering into
the eyes of her newborn
for the first time,
she was overcome with the immensity
of
this treasure,
the beautiful pearl
that now lay before her.

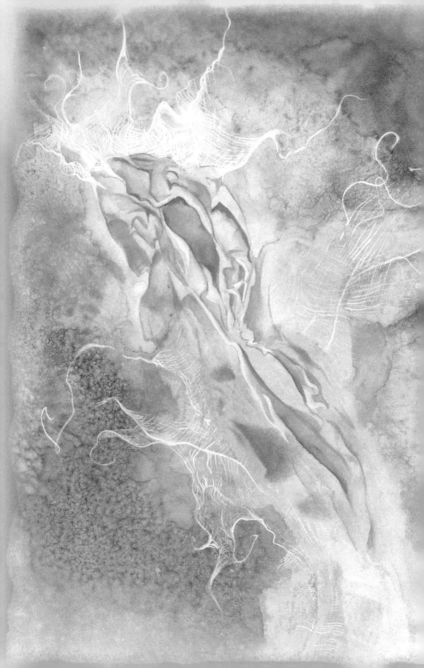

We began to understand
the treasure of
Faith,
understanding how our own misperceptions,
our own bitterness,
can entomb
Faith.
How illusion can spin a web around her,
like
a spider embalming its prey . . .

And just as the constant
wash of a wave,
will wear the craggiest of surfaces smooth,
Faith
she is relentless
in splaying herself
against our harsh edges.

It is
Faith
that washes us smooth, smooth so
that we may act
as reflections for one another.
And
Faith
she is sturdy in her knowing,
the knowing
that a smooth surface
casts a truer reflection,
than one mottled
with texture that distorts.

And just as a pearl
forms in response to the intrusion
of an abrading grain of sand,
it is
Faith
that
forms around our suffering,
to shield
the soft places in our soul . . .

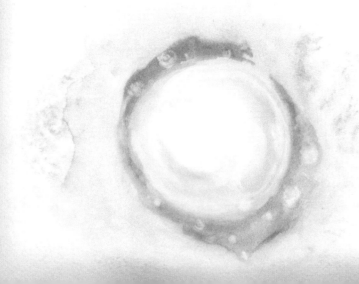

. . . And so it was
that we came to know,
this
pearl of great price,
this
was the gift
of
Faith.

Then
Joy
stepped forward,
swaying gently from side to side.
In the air hung a melody,
simple
like the morning cry of a wren.

She stood very still
as the melody emerged
like the dawn,
and then
with outstretched hands,
she beckoned to her companions.

They circled 'round
like ripples
that follow as a stone
descends into a pond.

As they each
took their place
beside her,
the music, it began to deepen.

No longer was it simple,
for within the joyful notes
were woven the somber
and within the heavy
were woven the light.

. . . And this
tapestry of sound . . .
it moved
to the cadence
of our souls.

Joy
turned herself upon us,
with outstretched hands.
She beckoned us forward,
and said simply,

. . . "Will you Dance?"

We stood
stunned and silent,
until once again
she asked,
with a voice as even as fresh fallen snow,

"Will you Dance?"

It was
at
that moment,
we each
made the choice
of who
we would be
in this lifetime.

And the
choice
it hovered above us . . .

as if
held
by an unseen hand.

Realization swept across us,
like
sea spray hitting warm summer skin.
And we
knew
from a place deep within us
that
to dance
with one,
was to dance
with all.

And we
knew
with quiet certainty
that
to forego the dance
and sit down in silence
was merely
to sit
in the shelter
of
a tomb which houses
a life
never fully lived . . .

In that moment

we

each

stood

alone.

The melody,
reached out for us,
like waves reaching out for the shoreline

and
there
we stood . . .

hearing
every
sound
we
had ever known . . .

the refuge of laughter . . .

the echo of grace . . .

. . . the haunting call of sorrow.

And
then
as if crossing

a   great   chasm

we gathered our strength within us
and
blindly
stepped over
the
edge

for we knew
that the dance
born of this struggle . . .

this was
the gift of
Joy . . .

And
We
Danced

We danced for moments,
and
we danced for lifetimes,
dancing
both our sorrow and our bliss.

We
danced
to hold on,

and we danced
to let go.

We danced
until
we were wise like an elder,
we danced
until
we were innocent like a child.

We danced until
we could
dance
no longer.

And then,
like
steam

revealing   itself   across   a   window

a dark
cloaked figure
emerged
on the edge
of our vision.

As he neared,
his hood dropped away,
revealing thick sterling hair,
that fell soft
like starlight against his neck . . .
and for a moment
Destiny
held us
in the
soft
black velvet
of his gaze.

Without words
he
gathered his disciples,
like a shepherd
would call
in his flock.

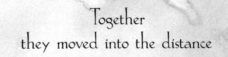

Together
they moved into the distance

growing faint like the chanting
of an ancient prayer.

And there we stood . . .

in
the
Doorway
of
Knowing . . .

each of us having been
crucified
by the darkness,
and baptized
by the light.

The future, it stretched before us
with arms wide like the sea . . .

. . . and we knew
from the quiet that fell upon us
that our dance,
for now,
it was done.

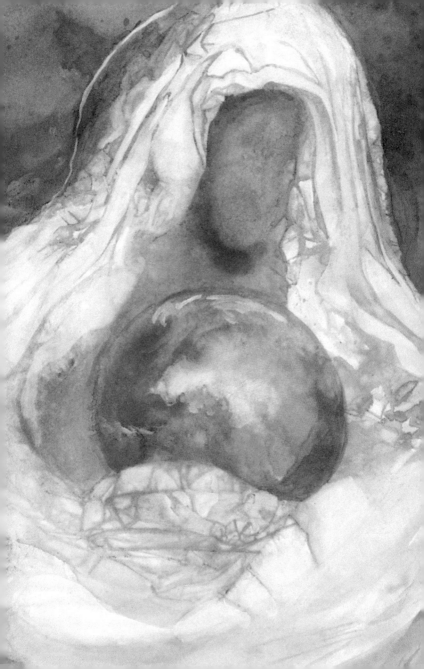

And
Peace
rocked us gently
in her arms
that night,
as we surrendered
to
sleep
spun like gold . . .

Afterword

There comes a time- it is often at midlife- when people, naturally turn their attention to the verities, the great, unresolved philosophical questions of existence. Does life have a meaning? Who am I ? Where do I come from? Where is it that I am going?

Annette Childs-Oroz has done the world a service by writing this book, a fine work of spiritual art, really. It is an inspiring allegory of struggle and renewal that will tug at the heart strings of anyone who has ever had to surmount a wrenching personal crisis of the spirit, or suffered an overwhelming personal loss, and that includes almost all of us who have lived at least a couple of decades.

Annette is a warm, sensitive, bright, and accomplished psychotherapist. She has devoted the bulk of her career to working with the dying and the bereaved, thus, her writing comes from a heartfelt understanding of the struggles that eventually plague us all.

I like her way of personifying the forces like "fear" and "change" that are always looming over each human life. It harks back to the eternally haunting tales that have come down to us through the ancient Greek myths. And to my way of thinking, using the sacred art of storytelling to tame these forces with which we all contend, is as good a way of dealing with them as any that has ever been devised.

Annette deserves praise for her accomplishment in this book. It is a work that will refresh its readers, and the message it contains is one that will stay with them for a very, very long time.

Raymond A. Moody, Jr., M.D., Ph.D

For ordering information or to correspond with the author please contact

THE
wandering
feather
PRESS

1-866-819-4133

Dr. Childs-Oroz is available for workshops and lectures.
For more information on Dr. Childs-Oroz' work,
or to schedule an event, see her website at

www.willyoudance.com

About the Artist

Karen Kreyeski's life is creating and teaching art to people of all ages. When Karen first read "Will You Dance?" she felt a deep connection to the book. Creating the pieces for this book was an odyssey of the spirit, as each of the characters introduced itself, demanding the right to be seen. Using various watercolor media the paintings each evolved as if having a life of their very own, resulting in the rich archetypal artwork which you see displayed in the pages of this book.

Karen's work is in various private collections in Nevada and Montana. She lives in the foothills of the Sierra Nevada Mountains, spending her days doing that which she loves.

About the Author

Annette Childs-Oroz holds a Ph.D. in psychology and maintains a private practice assisting individuals and families to grow through painful transitions. She has devoted much of her work to assisting the dying and their families to find peace and meaning at the end of life.

As a researcher she has extensively studied the positive after effects of the near death experience and other mystical phenomena, and has contributed original research to the field of near death studies.

Having been abundantly blessed with the companionship of a wonderful family and true friends, most days go by in a blur, lost to the happy chaos of a life being fully lived..